HEART POSTURES

For Hope, Healing , and Growth

Andrea M. Moore

To every heart longing to be held in the Father's hands.

INTRODUCTION

How's your heart?
Your responses may vary. You might make statements about your heart's physical capacity, your emotions , or what you do from your heart.

Have you considered that your heart's posture or attitude, toward God can determine how you process every moment of your life?

There is a grace available upon request from the Holy Spirit to guide us in processing each moment of our lives. It is accessed by giving God permission to promote His will for us. As we reach a place of abandon concerning our heart issues, we surrender ourselves as soft clay in the hands of the Potter.

The benefit is a progressive fulfillment of God's plan for our lives. When we give God the proper place in our lives- above, as well as front and center- He will take us from one state of glory to another.
My sincere prayer is that this book creates a space in your life for considering the status of your heart, provides biblically-based ways to heal from attacks on your heart, and inspires you to seek greater intimacy with God and His Word.

Acknowledgements

With deep gratitude and awe, I first acknowledge my Lord and Savior, Jesus Christ. A constant supply of His grace, mercy, and revelation made this book possible from initiation to completion.

I'm grateful to family members and friends who supported me during this process, especially:
My mother, Ella Moore, from whom I inherited my love for reading and writing.
My sister, Tina Howard, for always standing in my corner, cheering me on.
James and Donna Moore, my brother and sister-in-love for support,
and Lauren Watson, my beautiful daughter, who inspires me to be an example of how to walk surrendered before the Lord.

To those I call family at Purpose House Church, I appreciate you! To my leaders, Pastors Darin and Kristi Bray: thank you for your prayers and encouragement.

To my friends: Cheryl Frazier, Kim Rider, Susan Bailey, Connie Elliott, and Natisha Webb. Your friendship means more than I can adequately express.

To my editor: Mr. James Murray, thank you for recognizing the "heart" of this project.

Many thanks to Danielle Anderson for making the connection at the perfect time.

Jamie Crockett: thank you for the cover photo.

Last, but certainly not least, I thank Miss Sheria Stringer. Though you now rejoice in heaven, I have heard your voice in my heart, asking, "How's that book going?"

Look, Sheria – I finished the book!

Contents

Chapter 1

Guard Your Heart

"Above all else, guard your heart, for it is the wellspring of life." (NIV)
"Keep vigilant watch over your heart; it is where life starts." (MSG)

"Keep your heart with all diligence, for out of it spring the issues of life." (NKJV)

Regardless of the biblical translation, Proverbs 4:23 sends a clear message about protecting the heart. A closer look into the scripture gives practical insight as it relates to our hearts.

The phrase, "to watch" in Hebrew is "nasaw," meaning to guard or keep. To protect our hearts from danger.

Think about how we secure our homes with the latest technology: remote access, video surveillance, around-the-clock support. In efforts to keep undesirable situations from our homes, we are intentional. Spiritually we are also a "house" for the Holy Spirit. Our heart is the center of the house. A healthy heart is necessary to have an attitude toward God that cooperates with His will. God places invaluable treasures in our hearts to be nurtured for His purposes. They should be carefully protected.

In Hebrew, heart is "lebab." It defines our heart as the seat of the soul. We are three part beings: body, soul and spirit. When we receive the gift of the Holy Spirit, He resides in us. In the ideal scenario, our heart yields to the authority of the Holy Spirit. Emotions are a gift from God and can be very powerful. Emotions can easily mislead us. If we allow our heart and its emotions to be our base of operations, we create a breach in the security of our "house." An attack aimed at our emotions can deliver a blow from which we may find it difficult to recover. We cannot address spiritual issues at the level of our emotions. When we override our emotions and are guided by the Holy Spirit, we defeat weapons formed by the enemy and protect our hearts. Applying the authority of Jesus' name to our issues sets us up for victory.

"Shamar" in Hebrew means to keep watch over. Another admonishment to keep constant guard over our hearts. To guard with keen personal interest, as if our lives depend on it. I envision a constant, non-stop, IHOP, 7-Eleven, no rest type of guarding! The kind that only God is capable of, because He neither slumbers or sleeps. This thwarts the enemy's strategy of hurling a constant stream of assaults targeted at our hearts.

The issues of life. Our world. Our life history. Our story. How we see our lives, others and situations. Our personal history is the filter through which we experience God. Issues of life set the stage for the quality of character we demonstrate during every mountain top and valley experience.

The good news, the news of the Gospel, is that we have the victory! When Jesus died and was raised again from the dead, He defeated sin, death and the works of the enemy. For us. Forever. God fixed the fight, Jesus won the victory—so WE WIN! Nevertheless, it's necessary to regularly check the status of our hearts. Heart checks keep our thoughts and attitudes in alignment with God's heart. We partner with Him and discover how to walk in God's will. We cooperate with the Holy Spirit as the gatekeeper of our hearts. The wisdom of the Holy Spirit directs us in determining what is worthy of occupancy in our hearts. We will discern if we have let something reside in our hearts that needs to be released or if we need to embrace a truth that we let slip away. Faulty gate-keeping can harm our hearts. Damaged hearts are out of alignment with a surrendered position to the One who can strengthen, heal, and make it whole.

Heart Check

Pause and ask the Holy Spirit to reveal any areas of your life where you have not surrendered to God's leading. Have you "over" or "under" guarded your heart?

Chapter 2
Getting Connected

The best way to know more about God and be led by His Spirit is to know what He says. We do this by reading the Bible. It's like connective heart tissue, creating a path from Him to us. Each time we open the Word of God, and ask the Holy Spirit to give us understanding of what we read, the connection gets stronger and deeper. We invite ourselves into a conversation with Him. We open the door to encounter God and give Him permission to remove what holds our hearts hostage. Applying the truths of God's Word to our hearts initiates the process of revelation. God begins to reveal the truth of His Word to us. The leading of the Holy Spirit was never meant to be a special occasion. God sent us the gift of the Holy Spirit as a daily expectation.

As intimacy increases, our trust in Him expands and the revelation of His Word becomes our base of operations. From a foundation of knowing and trusting God, we process the highs and lows of life. We take part in God's unlimited heart exchange program. He transplants His ways into our heart. We lay down our preferences and embrace God's. We surrender our:

- Thoughts
- Plans
- Decisions
- Desires
- Expectations

for His.

View the heart postures in this book through the lens of this precious connective tissue. Position yourself for an encounter, for a heart exchange. The Bible has no disclaimers, or addendums. It says who God is and will always be to us and for us. It also defines who we are to Him.

Heart Check

Have you seen reading the Bible as a conversation
with God? If yes, how? If no, why?

Chapter 3

Heart Attacks

Heart attacks.

These are attempts to have our hearts disconnect with the truth
of God's Word and our true identity in Christ. They affect our
soul: our mind, will and emotions. Attacks disrupt our thoughts
and feelings and influence our behavior. Stealing our identity in
Christ, killing our call, and destroying our destiny in God are
some of the reasons for heart attacks. John 10:10 reminds us that
although the enemy devises plans of attack, Jesus came so that we
have life, and have it to its fullest measure. Assaults on our hearts
can enter our lives without provocation. Our personal history
may include events that we could not control but the experience
wounded our hearts. Disobedience to God's leading can also find

us dealing with heart injuries. The focus in the chapters that follow won't be on the many reasons but on the resulting heart posture. If it causes us to turn toward or away from God.

Every posture may not immediately resonate with you, and that's okay. As you read each profile, pause to ask the Holy Spirit, "Is this a posture I hold in my heart?" Use the postures and the "heart checks" that follow as a template for a spiritual tune up. As we grow with God, the enemy may try a new tact targeting our hearts. Routinely taking spiritual inventory helps us to guard our hearts. God's eternal truths defeat every scheme of the enemy. Regular "checks" give us direction on how and where to apply these truths.

The introspection required to participate in the heart checks in this book do not require a theology degree or a lifetime of church attendance. However, it takes courage and honesty to consider how you have been filtering the events of your life through your heart. It may sting a bit to make the admissions, but every confession will be heard by a loving and forgiving God. A God that has very specific, prosperous plans for your success.

Heart Check

Holy Spirit: are there subtle attacks that I haven't acknow-
ledged that are influencing the way I see God? Which attacks
that are easy to identify?

Chapter 4

A Broken Heart

Jeannie is a beautiful blond with dancing eyes and a ready smile. You would be surprised to know that her history includes being sexually assaulted by a family member over a period of 5 years starting at the age of seven. It changed everything she knew about trust, safety, authority, love, self-esteem and more. It's like a hidden disease that gets triggered at different times in her life. It's hard for Jeannie to trust the others, especially authority figures.

Something happened. A boundary was crossed, trust was violated. A stable, secure part of your heart, your life was dismantled by a painful circumstance. This posture can be experienced at any age and repeatedly. It may be due to abuse or neglect. Rejection, betrayal, or loss could be the culprit. Even witnessing trauma can create a fissure.

Deep healing is needed for this heart to beat with hope, trust, and faith in God again. There is a risk of living life in rejection, fear, offense, self-hatred, anger, depression, shame, or anxiety, without realizing it. Much of life with others is spent in self-preservation mode instead of seeking true connection. The infection from this wound in their heart is the filter through which they process the motives and intentions of others including God. It may be hard to believe that God loves and cares for them with unconditional, everlasting love. A question held in this heart may be "How could you have let this happen to me?" Bitter or gun-shy prayers can come from this posture, inwardly wondering if their heart's longings are worthy to present to God.

Healing from this posture involves deliverance from the bondage and negative attachments that came as a result of the violation. You may feel as if your life has been held hostage by the intense pain that has taken root in a broken heart.

When we tell God - without fear, all about our broken heart, He will take care of every detail. God heals by revealing His truth to us. The truth about how He values us and how we can find identity, worth, and security in Him. If we choose His truth over the facts of our lives, we begin to repair the broken places in our thinking and feeling processes. One crucial truth to remember is that our identities are not what happened to us. Our identities and hopes are in Christ Jesus, not the attacks our hearts endured.

Heart Check

Lord, am I identifying with any trauma in my life more than I'm identifying myself as being your beloved? Show me the places where I'm bound so I can seek total healing in Your name.

Chapter 5

A Rejected Heart

Tanya is always good. Not a person who knows her would disagree. She's helpful, generous, productive and successful. In her heart, she's used this as a protective strategy. Growing up, messages from teachers, loved ones and those in authority established that she was not valuable. She had to do MORE of everything to be worthy of love and attention. So she worked—hard. She tried—hard. Everything needed to be hard to be "enough." Her internal value is at the mercy of those around her. Her mood is also attached to her "performance" in life. If she is good and performs well, she's happy and avoids rejection from others.

This heart attack is aimed at our universal, innate desire to be accepted, loved and valued. Rejection can hit at the core of what makes us feel special and unique. This attack comes after our identity. It makes a big impact considering our performance-driven culture.

In our world we are celebrated, honored, even loved based on what we can produce outside of ourselves. We become our ability to perform. Our identity becomes performance-based instead of relational. This posture discounts the value of our adoption into the body of Christ. In doing so, the determination of our value is made by others instead of an omniscient, loving God.
When we don't get the acceptance we desire, we can feel insignificant and rejected. This mindset gives permission to others to determine our importance. A rejected heart is usually surrounded by protective walls of pride, anger, even manufactured joy to avoid encountering the sting of rejection.

There is a very real fear of encountering situations that resemble the last incident with rejection. This may bring on a preemptive attack on others. Few threaten the security of a rejected heart and come out unscathed.

This heart heals through the exercise of casting down imaginations compiled from serial rejection. Freedom from the bondage of placing faith in the opinions of people will shift perspective. True healing comes when our foundational identity and value are based on the unchanging Word of God.

Here is the truth, rejected heart: if you have a heartbeat, you have a purpose! This purpose was determined by God before your great-great-grandmother's father was born. Every detail of your life was joyously pre-planned to equip you with God-given value that cannot be reversed, reduced, or repossessed by another unless we give them permission. Meditation on God's Word will renew the mind and heart of the rejected to its true and eternal value.

Heart Check

Holy Spirit, highlight any imaginations that I'm holding higher than the truth that I am loved and adopted by God. Show me any deep-seated false beliefs I hold that have me striving for Your love instead of simply resting and receiving.

_____
_____
_____
_____
_____
_____
_____

Chapter 6

A Distracted Heart

Hello: my name is Andrea and I have lived a life steeped in distraction! Distraction is part of my personal story. I allowed societal expectations, the opinions of others and a preference for avoidance to lead me down the road to distraction. The comparison trap that I fell into sold me the lie that busy and striving is better. Living an overworked and over-scheduled life leaves contemplative time by the wayside. I majored in this heart posture for years, choosing performance to measure my value.

A distracted heart will have a person majoring in the minors in the spirit. This continuation in error leads to distracted thoughts, prayers, distracted spiritual warfare, and distracted declarations. This heart can truly love God but lacks consistency with focusing on things concerning God. The concerns of the world and the lust of the eyes and life have taken center stage. A person with this heart works God into its life instead of making God the center of everything. Walking in a distracted posture robbed me of spiritual growth and authority. Intentionally seeking God's kingdom first by prioritizing God's Word and presence over my "To Do" list was a way I adjusted my posture. Developing a firm foundational knowledge of God's covenant with me fueled the hunger to pursue more of God on a daily basis.

Heart Check

Holy Spirit: Show me any activity in my life that is distracting me from Your Word and/or Your presence. Give me a fresh hunger and thirst to seek the Kingdom of God first.

_____

_____

_____

_____

_____

_____

Chapter 7

A Hardened Heart

Nick was fine until people started talking about how wonderful God is and His unconditional love. Nick thought, "Anyone with half a brain can tell that those stories in the Bible are fairy tales. If God was so good why did He let his alcoholic dad beat his mother every day and then leave?" To make things worse, his mother kept on picking men like his dad who continued the pattern of violence in his childhood. Who needs a God that plays favorites? A God that can't stop a sloppy drunk? Nick decided that only what he could see, hear, and control was real. Who needs hope? You only wind up disappointed.

Apathy or indifference is also a decision of the heart. A heart "attack" due to unmet expectations and disappointment can cause us to hold offense in our hearts.

Here is the possible progression:
Sustained offense can lead to prolonged anger, which leads to resentment and bitterness. This results in a hardened heart. Hardening in the heart, no matter how small, keeps us from fully being a demonstration of God's love for others. His plans to use us as instruments of His love and grace are limited by what we are carrying in our hearts. This is an insidious attack because often we are responding to something that was done to us that planted the seed of offense. Few people wake in the morning deciding to be a walking demonstration of offense to the world. It is a self-preservation response to unresolved pain. Even with successful repression and denial, bitterness is challenged in the presence of the unconditional nature of God. So the approach to God comes from a victimized posture, not a victorious one. A hard heart

loses sight of the fact that Jesus has secured the victory for us. This is hard to grasp in our valley seasons. Searching the Bible for God's promises can realign us to those truths and not the pain of disappointment. During this process, we will encounter the gift of forgiveness, which will break us free from the prison of our pain. It does not invalidate the painful experience but it releases the vice grip that it has on your destiny. Operating in forgiveness will clear out bitterness taking up territory in our hearts.

Heart Check

Holy Spirit, show me the situations that cause me to host bitterness in my heart. Soften the places in my heart that have become hardened. Give me Your grace to forgive others the way You have forgiven me. I replace bitterness with love.

```
------------------------------------------------------------
------------------------------------------------------------
------------------------------------------------------------
------------------------------------------------------------
------------------------------------------------------------
------------------------------------------------------------
------------------------------------------------------------
```

Chapter 8

A Divided Heart

Anthony grew up in the church. He was the closest you could get to a PK (Preacher's Kid). He was the child of a dedicated church leader. If the church was open, he and his family were there. Well, even if it wasn't, because they had the keys! As Anthony got older, he found himself in different circles of influence. In some circles, his church-going background was an advantage- in others not as much. He deftly lifestyle- switched depending on his company. He got so used to it that he stopped noticing when it was happening. When he needed guidance and sound advice he had many options but no direction.

The divided heart has decided to straddle the commitment fence. It is successful for brief periods of time. This heart leans partially on the worldly rationale and partially on God's Word if it fits the motives at hand. The hallmark of a divided heart is emotional instability. One day all is right with the world, and by night-fall, everything is in shambles. This heart depends on a certain amount of self- righteousness that may or may not appear arrogant.

Their own idolized opinions become the ladder they climb to get closer to Jesus. A major pitfall with this posture is that one failure from striving is a deathblow to identity and causes confusion.

This heart, even after considering the restorative work of Christ determines that it is not quite enough to cover their situation. They consider it too great for the atoning blood of Christ. A divided heart is both a grateful recipient of God's grace and also exalts their own judgment and ideas above the finality of God's Word.

Trust issues need to be resolved to correct this posture. There may also be a fear of losing control, status and/or popularity. A divided heart can wear itself out trying to earn spiritual "extra credit." People-pleasing may be a strategy to substitute for God's guidance.
Confession, surrender to the unconditional nature of God's love, and humility heals this heart. Completely applying God's covenant to every area in life will lay a foundation that will bring peace and stability.

Heart Check

Holy Spirit, are there areas in my life where I am depending on my limited understanding instead of You? Show me how to lean on you totally for wisdom and understanding.

_____

_____

_____

_____

_____

_____

Chapter 9

Our Hope in the Story of David

Don't despair if you saw yourself in all of the postures explored in previous chapters. There's hope! We can simultaneously find ourselves in heart postures turning us to God and ones where our hearts need to grow closer to Him. We can be dealing with one of the heart "attacks" described AND demonstrate the presence-seeking postures that follow. You can be experiencing a broken heart and praise sincerely from a worshipful heart. Postures are not mutually exclusive. Heart postures are either rooted in fear or love. Postures based on fear and pain move us away from God. Those based on love turn our hearts to Him.

A Biblical example of coexisting heart postures is King David. He had a bold and courageous heart before being anointed by the prophet Samuel. David honored and feared God. His heart was in unadulterated pursuit of God. As the author of the majority of the book of Psalms, you can almost hear his heart cries: for God to come for comfort, strength, and wisdom.

Though David's accomplishments in God were larger than life, he was one that erred in the sight of God. He abused his power in order to commit adultery and murder. Even with these significant moral failings, David did not lose his status as one after God's heart.

David demonstrated a reconciliatory posture toward God on a regular basis. He was honest and open about his sin, repented often and endured the judgment of God, even to the point of suffering the death of his son. In Psalm 51, he cried out to God, "create in me a clean heart, renew a steadfast spirit within me!" He understood that he was dependent on the grace and mercies of God to move past his poor judgement.

Some of you may be reading this who have one or more transgressions in common with David. I repeat—there is hope for you because God is bigger than your sin. He is bigger than the guilt and shame you carry attached to your choices. His love overshadows any condemnation. It's crucial for you to understand that heart realignment requires honesty and an acceptance that there are consequences but not condemnation from God when we repent for sinful behavior. The gift of repentance opens the door to greater intimacy with God.

As we consider these next intimacy-seeking postures, keep in mind that you may experience more than one at a given time. Some postures will be more pronounced depending on what God is developing in you at a given time.

Chapter 10

The Open Heart

Sydney wasn't against God, participating in organized Christianity just was not a priority in her life. Her father was the one who went to church on most Sundays. It was optional for her since Mom stayed home. She decided to attend some services with her father out of curiosity. After four visits, Sydney had an impact encounter with the presence of God. As a result, she genuinely felt known and loved by God. This created a hunger in Sydney to seek her own intimate relationship with God.

An open heart comes to the realization that an intimate, personal relationship is possible. A desire is kindled in this heart, fueled by the realization that God is an accessible, "hands-on" God. This requires laying down any preconceived notions about the dynamics of God's character. An open heart embraces the truth that our God is a God of relationship. This posture eliminates the distance between God's heart and theirs. Inviting God to see their heart and starting the journey to discover His.

Heart Check

Holy Spirit, how can I open my heart more to being "known" by God? Are there places I'm hiding? What preconceived ideas am I holding onto about God?

_____
_____
_____
_____
_____
_____

Chapter 11
A Listening Heart

I'll share my personal story about listening to God. To know that you are actively listening first requires an awareness that someone is speaking. Up until approximately 10 years ago, I had virtually no knowledge of hearing from God. As a child, my family didn't attend church regularly, but we did say grace, nighttime prayers, and went to church on Easter Sunday.

God started to speak to me by making me sensitive to the feelings of others. My mother would say that I looked out for the "underdog." I didn't realize that it was the Holy Spirit speaking to me until I was an adult. I enjoyed listening to people's stories and later wanted to help others by praying for them. Then I began to experience what I call disruptive God thoughts. They were too amazing and impactful to others to be my own! That created a desire to hear more. It became the foundation for developing my listening heart posture.

A listening heart sets the stage for the postures that require you to lean into and onto God. May we never lose our desire to listen to the heart of God! He is speaking His heart to us in every situation, from the seemingly inconsequential to the life-altering.

In this posture, we hear the voice of God over all others vying for attention, including our own soulful voices. We heed the direction of that voice. Following God instead of moving ahead with our own plans and later asking God to meet us there with His grace. Or bail us out. We become sheep of the Shepherd—recognizing His voice. Ready to reap the benefits promised in Psalm 23. How do we get there, you ask? We become familiar with His voice. You can hear it reading the Bible, during prayer, during worship, and quiet moments of intimate adoration. Listening doesn't happen in a vacuum, life is happening all around us. We have to be intentional, choosing time to be with God. We clear life's clutter first, removing what keeps us from hearing His voice.

One issue may be a false sense of urgency. We think we have to make that phone call, say yes to that invitation, accept that new responsibility. All of these things are good in moderation and with balance. However, if left unchecked, all of our time is spoken for and our hearts' meditations are scattered among many issues.

A listening heart has an ear to hear about the new hope for its life instead of working God into its personal agenda. In this posture, you make yourself available to hear the truth of God's Word so it can penetrate the heart. Even a frustrated heart can muster enough hope to give God a try to see if there will be real change. It is a step to which God responds. The evidence of His response is increased faith, peace and supernatural revelation in our lives.

Heart Check

Holy Spirit, am I a good listener to Your small still voice and Your mighty roar? Turn my attention to any places in my life where I have decided to listen to the voices competing with Yours.

Chapter 12

A Faithful Heart

Vincent was young and successful by the world's standards. He grew up going to church but grew disenchanted when he saw so-called church leaders live one life on Sunday and another on Monday. How was God continuing to let these moral failures influence entire congregations? Following God was not what Vincent thought it should be. At least he was a good person! Then life happened. He had a questionable lab result. Considering the possibility of a life-changing diagnosis, Vincent began thinking of the God of his childhood. He returned to his Bible as a stabilizing force. By rekindling his hunger for the Word, Vincent put his trust in the promises of God. He was able to see past his circumstances to the faithfulness of God.

A faithful heart is easy to come by when the facts, details, and circumstances of our lives are favorable. With no perceived clouds of impending doom over our heads, we can easily behold the awesomeness of God. Enter stage left—irritation, frustration, unmet expectations, stress, relationship issues—and it's not long before we think that God has gone on vacation. Even with the ups and downs in life, a faithful heart remains stable with the right perspective. Philippians 4:6 and Philippians 4:8 give us a one-two punch on perspective, remembering the promise and person of God. Philippians 4:8 is a shortlist of God's top qualities: true, noble, etc. The report of Jesus IS the good news of the Gospel. When our faithfulness toward God is based on the character of God and not our present circumstances, we can believe when His Word tells us that He will never lie or fail us. Then we can approach God from a place of faith in our hearts. There is no need to spend time on (re)introductions. We already know who He is and who He is personally to us. There is no tug of war between your preference and God's will. The response is obedience to God's leading.

> **Heart Check**
> Holy Spirit: do I really know and trust All aspects of God's character? Am I leaning on my own preferences instead of trusting God's direction? Am I taking God personally? Where is my faith level?

Chapter 13

A Surrendered Heart

Genetria liked order. Never a fan of surprises, she had her own ideas about God. She decided to open her heart one night during Bible study. Silently, she said to God, I believe your Word is true but why can't I hear you NOW- when I need it the most? I've been faithful, but nothing's changed. In fact, some things have gotten worse! Genetria reasoned, God gave me this mind, so I'll figure out a solution. After a series of failed solutions, she continued her conversation with God. Being led to scriptures about faith, she came to the understanding that faith isn't faith if you can see it. She changed her question from why isn't this happening to asking how to partner with God as He was preparing her for His promise. She surrendered her "how and "why" to God and trusted Him with timing. This shifted her heart from anxious anticipation to joyful expectation.

The surrendered heart seeks alignment with God's will. This heart has come to the understanding that the best way is the way that God is leading. Proverbs 3:5-6 becomes the meditation of their heart. Trusting God and not leaning on their own understanding. This heart-set keeps us partnered with the Spirit of God. A surrendered heart has come to the realization that it is not by human might, intellect, or power but by the Spirit that God's eternal plans are accomplished. The surrendered heart seeks God for His strategic will in circumstances instead of lifting a prayer of complaint- offering God options of what He should do to solve their issues. Seeking God's wisdom is no longer a last resort, it is our first response. A surrendered heart has moved forward in faith- past emotions and trusts that God is who He says He is: the Great I am. During prayer, worship and even quiet moments of studying the Word this heart is open to the Holy Spirit taking over the situation.

Heart Check

Holy Spirit, are there places in my life where I feel more secure leaning on my own understanding? Show me where I'm striving and teach me how to rest and partner with Your perfect will.

_____
_____

Conclusion

Now what?

The postures mentioned in this book are not an exhaustive listing. My hope is that exploring the status of your heart created an awareness of how life's circumstances can turn our hearts toward seeking God or away from God's truth about our identity in Him and His love for us.

To maintain postures that create a God-shaped heart, continue regular heart checks. Enlist the help of a trusted, believing friend for accountability. Meet with your spiritual leadership if you are a member of a church. This is especially critical during tough times. Traumatic experiences can create moments where we could choose to be shaped by our circumstances instead of the truths of the Bible. Consider this book a reference to keep your heart and mind rooted in the truth of God's word. Circumstances are FACTS but the TRUTH is what God says about them.

May you experience the gift of healing revelation from the Spirit of God as you continue your heart journey.

Notes:

Notes:

ABOUT THE AUTHOR

Andrea M. Moore

Andrea is a writer, speaker and teacher with a passion to see others emotionally and spiritually transformed by the truths of God's Word. She develops teachings to create safe spaces that promote revelation, healing and growth. As a devoted student of  the Bible, she seeks to apply scriptural principles to the challenges of everyday living. Andrea desires to see others healed and fully equipped to move forward in their unique, God-given destinies.

Made in the USA
Columbia, SC
12 December 2020

27497088R00024